0500000077390 8

JB Sta
Zuehlke, Jeffrey, 1968-
Joseph Stalin

Joseph STALIN

Jeffrey Zuehlke

Twenty-First Century Books
Minneapolis

For the twenty million

Twenty-First Century Books
A division of Lerner Publishing Group
241 First Avenue North
Minneapolis, MN 55401 U.S.A.

Website address: www.lernerbooks.com

Library of Congress Cataloging-in-Publication Data

Zuehlke, Jeffrey, 1968–
  Joseph Stalin / by Jeffrey Zuehlke.
    p.   cm. — (A&E biography)
  Includes bibliographical references and index.
  ISBN-13: 978–0–8225–3421–1 (lib. bdg. : alk. paper)
  ISBN-10: 0–8225–3421–5 (lib. bdg. : alk. paper)
  1. Stalin, Joseph, 1879–1953—Juvenile literature. 2. Heads of state—Soviet Union—Biography—Juvenile literature. 3. Soviet Union—History—1925–1953—Juvenile literature. I. Title. II. Biography (Lerner Publications Company)
DK268.S8Z84 2006
947.084'2'092—dc22   2005011900

Manufactured in the United States of America
1 2 3 4 5 6 – BP – 11 10 09 08 07 06

CONTENTS

Soviet dictator Joseph Stalin in 1952, one year before his sudden death

PROLOGUE: DEATH OF A TYRANT

March 1, 1953. The housekeeping and security staff were nervous. It was getting late in the afternoon, and Comrade Joseph Stalin, their boss and the leader of the Union of Soviet Socialist Republics (USSR, or Soviet Union), had yet to emerge from his apartment. He should have awakened hours ago, but his rooms showed no signs of life.

As the hours passed, Stalin's staff realized something was wrong. The Boss, as they called him, never slept so late. Still, they dared not disturb him. Stalin had given strict orders to never come into his apartment without his permission. He feared an assassin might sneak in and try to kill him while he slept. The staff knew that disobeying their boss's orders would probably mean imprisonment, if not execution. Yet if the Boss was ill and needed help, failure to assist him might also cost them their lives.

Finally, at 10:30 P.M., one of the security officers, Peter Lozgachev, decided to go in. About forty years later, Lozgachev described the moment. "As a rule, we were careful not to creep up on him. . . . He reacted badly if you went into his rooms quietly. I opened the door and walked noisily along the corridor . . . and there was the Boss lying on the floor holding up his right hand."

The seventy-four-year-old leader of the world's largest country had a look of terror on his face. He tried to speak but could only make a dull buzzing sound. He was lying in a pool of his own urine.

Someone called Stalin's top officials to tell them of the situation. The staff waited impatiently for hours before Lavrenty Beria, head of state security, and Georgy Malenkov, Stalin's deputy, finally showed up. They looked at the Boss. He clearly looked ill, but he appeared to be resting comfortably. "Beria swore at me," Lozgachev recalled. "Beria said to me: 'Don't cause a panic, don't bother us.' Then they left."

By 8 A.M. on March 2, Stalin had shown no signs of recovery. Another Soviet official, Nikita Khrushchev, appeared and called in a medical team. But Stalin's best doctors—including his personal physician who had treated him for years—were all in prison. While the leader lay ill, his doctors were being tortured by secret police agents in order to force them to confess to crimes they had not committed.

A short time later, a new team of doctors arrived. "[They] . . . were all terrified," Lozgachev recalled. "They had to examine him, but their hands were shaking."

The doctors made a diagnosis: Stalin had suffered a massive stroke—a loss of blood to his brain. The frightened doctors tried several treatments, but Stalin showed no signs of recovery. One doctor summed up the situation: "Death is inevitable."

Over the four days, a crowd began to gather in

Joseph Stalin lies in state after his death in March 1953.

Stalin's apartment. Beria, Malenkov, and Khrushchev kept a close eye on Stalin, waiting to see if he would recover. In recent months, their boss had become increasingly suspicious of them. They knew that Stalin was probably making plans to arrest them. They would be forced to confess to crimes against the government. Once they confessed, they would be executed.

Stalin's death would save their lives. According to a witness, Beria looked triumphant when Stalin was unconscious. But his expression changed to grave concern during the periods when the Boss opened his eyes.

At 9:50 P.M. on March 5, 1953, Joseph Stalin died. During his nearly twenty-five years as the leader of the Soviet Union, he had concentrated total power in his hands. He led the country in the name of Communism—a system of government and economics that promised a paradise on earth, where all citizens would be equal, and every person's needs would be met. And in the name of Communism, he waged war on his own people, engineering the deaths of about twenty million.

Joseph was born in this house in Gori, Georgia, in 1878 or 1879.

Chapter **ONE**

GEORGIAN

THE MAN WHO WOULD LATER BECOME JOSEPH STALIN was born Iosif (Joseph) Vissarionovich Dzhugashvili in the town of Gori in the country of Georgia. Like many facts about Stalin's early life, his exact birth date is a matter of dispute. Most sources list his date of birth as December 21, 1879. But records uncovered after the collapse of the Soviet Union in 1991 show Stalin to have been born on December 18, 1878. Why Stalin chose to portray himself as a year younger is unclear, but throughout his rule, he frequently reconstructed history to suit his needs.

Joseph grew up as an only child, the son of Vissarion (nicknamed Beso) and Yekaterina (Keke) Dzhugashvili. Joseph's father was a shoemaker. His mother, a deeply religious Christian, washed laundry and repaired clothes. The Dzhugashvilis lived in a small, damp, fifteen-square-foot room in a shack on the poor side of town.

The Dzhugashvili household was often violent. Joseph's father was an alcoholic who flew into terrible rages when drunk. An eyewitness to these episodes described one many years later. "One day when his father was drunk he picked [Joseph] up and threw him violently to the floor. There was blood in the

Joseph's mother, Keke, in the late 1800s. Beso, Joseph's father, was not kind to Joseph and Keke, often beating both of them.

boy's urine for days afterward." Beso also beat Joseph's mother.

Sometimes during her husband's rages, Keke would fight back. Accounts suggest that the strong-willed Keke often won these fights. She "thrashed him mercilessly," according to Stalin. This is perhaps the reason why, when Joseph was still a child, Beso moved to the nearby capital city of Tiflis to work in a shoe factory.

Life without his violent father was not much easier for Joseph. Said one eyewitness, "His mother was the head of the family now, and the fist which had subdued his father was now applied to the upbringing of the son. She beat him unmercifully for disobedience."

Joseph grew up to be a cruel and angry person. A childhood friend described him as "incapable of feeling pity for man or beast. Even as a child he greeted the joys and [troubles] of his fellow schoolboys with a sarcastic smile. I never saw him cry." "His harsh home life left him embittered," a friend of Keke's said. "[Joseph] was an embittered, insolent, rude, stubborn child. . . . "

As a boy, Joseph's mean streak found release in throwing stones at birds and during his favorite game, *krivi*. This is a kind of large-scale boxing match, during which many kids would take sides and fight. "We pummeled each other unmercifully," one of Joseph's schoolmates recalled, "and weedy little [Joseph] was one of the craftiest scrappers. He had the knack of popping up unexpectedly behind a stronger opponent."

GROOMED FOR THE PRIESTHOOD

Joseph was a very bright student. He learned quickly and had an amazing ability to memorize and recite long passages from books. When Joseph was ten, Keke enrolled him in the Gori Church School. Her dream—and expectation—was that her son would become a priest. Her firm hand made sure he studied hard, and he earned excellent grades.

Joseph became the leader of a group of the strongest boys in his class. He was also very proud and became enraged when he thought he had been insulted.

At some point during Joseph's time at the Gori Church School, he became ill from smallpox, a sometimes-fatal infectious disease that causes fever and a severe skin

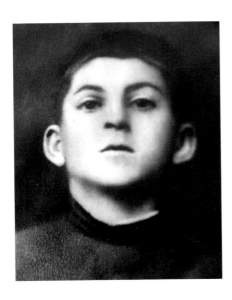

This photograph of Joseph was taken during the time he attended the Gori Church School. While at school, he earned good grades, but he also showed a tendency to be mean, even cruel.

rash. He missed many days of school because of the illness, and it left his skin scarred with pockmarks.

Joseph also suffered from a deformed left arm. It was shorter than his right arm and did not bend properly at the elbow. The fingers of his left hand were stiff and clumsy.

The arm problem may have been caused by blood poisoning. Joseph had been injured when he was run over by a cart. Although the accident did not appear to do any permanent damage, the blood poisoning that resulted may have caused his withered and deformed arm.

Joseph grew to a height of only five feet four inches, and he was self-conscious about his size. But despite his small frame, he was still strong and physically fit. Keke described him at the age of fifteen as "one of the strongest boys you ever saw." And whatever his physical stature, Joseph was an intimidating person. Most descriptions of him make note of his unusual eyes, which were often described as "yellow" and "tigerish."

Joseph finished his studies at the Gori Church School at or near the top of his class in July 1894. His mother, still expecting her son to become a priest, had found him a spot at the Tiflis Theological Seminary (religious school) in Georgia's capital city.

The Tiflis seminary was Georgia's leading academic institution. It was housed in a handsome building within Tiflis. Russian historian Edvard Radzinsky describes Tiflis at the time as "a beautiful, merry, drunken, sunwashed city." But the students—all boys—spent little time in the capital. They lived within the school, "walled in from that southern city brimful of temptations." They studied religious scriptures as well as Greek, Latin, and Russian.

Life at the seminary was dull. The days were filled with hours of intensive classroom study. Occasionally students were allowed to walk around the city for a short while, but the school's gates were closed at night.

Students were only allowed to read books approved by the school authorities, mostly religious texts. Books discussing politics, philosophy, or other nonreligious subjects were strictly forbidden. "We felt like prisoners, forced to spend our young lives in this place though innocent," recalled one of Stalin's classmates.

The miserable environment led many students to rebel against the school authorities. By his second year, young Joseph had become the leader of a group of boys who read illegal books and discussed forbidden topics, such as European philosophy and Charles Darwin's controversial theory of evolution. This theory posed the idea that all living things are related. It suggests that humankind was descended from apes, not from Adam and Eve, as told in the Bible.

At some point during his time at Tiflis, Joseph rejected Christianity. He became an atheist and came to hate religion and his religious schoolmasters. "There is no God, they [the teachers] are deceiving us," he told a classmate.

Joseph in school uniform at Tiflis Theological Seminary in 1894. He began his studies as an excellent student who enjoyed writing poetry, but exposure to radical ideas gave him a new purpose in life—revolution.

But this hatred for authority, shared by Stalin and his rebellious friends, was not just directed at their teachers and Christianity. It spilled over into politics and political ideas. In fact, the Tiflis seminary was a hotbed for radical politics. Much of the rebellion was directed against the ruling Russian government.

THE RUSSIAN EMPIRE AND RUSSIFYING GEORGIA

When Joseph was young, Georgia was part of the vast Russian Empire, which spanned from eastern Europe to the North Pacific Coast of Asia. The Russians had conquered Georgia through a series of wars during the early part of the nineteenth century. The Russian Empire was an autocracy, meaning the Russian czar, or emperor, held complete control over the government and the population. Russia had been ruled by the Romanov dynasty (family of rulers) for nearly three hundred years.

While many European countries had begun to experiment with limited forms of democracy in the nineteenth century, Russia had no elected government. Citizens had few rights and little freedom to express their beliefs or opinions. The czar's secret police arrested people suspected of holding anti-czarist views. Czarist authorities usually exiled (banished) such revolutionaries to the frozen wastelands of Siberia in northern and eastern Russia for years.

Most of Russia's wealth was controlled by a small class of landowners. These privileged few enjoyed an

Starving under czarist rule, this Russian peasant is leading his pony to be slaughtered for food for his family.

extravagant lifestyle. They lived on huge estates and attended elaborate balls and court ceremonies. But the vast majority of the czar's subjects were desperately poor and lived in miserable conditions.

While Joseph was at Tiflis, the Russian government was trying to "Russify" Georgia. Russian officials were installed in top government posts. The Russian language (as opposed to the native language, Georgian) was taught in schools. Russian teachers stressed that Russian culture was superior to Georgian ways. These policies were carried out to make Georgia an obedient state of the Russian Empire. But in many circles, such programs only intensified widespread hatred of Russia and czarist rule.

REVOLUTIONARIES AND MARXISM

As Joseph explored writings forbidden by the seminary teachers, he discovered one author who made a particularly strong impression on him. He was a German-born economist whose works, published in previous decades, were taking Europe by storm. His name was Karl Marx (1818–1883).

Marx's theories, collectively known as Marxism, seemed fresh, exciting, and ominous. Marx, in works such as *The Communist Manifesto* (cowritten with Friedrich Engels) and *Das Kapital,* claimed to have come to some gripping conclusions about the future of the world. He predicted that the world's Western capitalist societies (the United States, Germany,

France, Great Britain, and others), in which a hand-ful of rich men controlled almost all industry and wealth, would eventually be overthrown by their workers, the proletariat. The result of this revolution would be Socialism, a system of government in which most industry and property is owned by the public, not by individuals. Under Socialism, Marx wrote, every citizen's needs would be met and poverty would be abolished.

Taking his theory further, Marx predicted that Socialism would eventually transform itself into Com-munism. Under Communism, the proletariat would rule itself. The need for government would vanish, and the world would become a worker's paradise, in which all citizens would be equal and everything nec-essary would be provided for them. According to Marx, these changes were inevitable.

To young men like Joseph, Marx's ideas, especially his promise of a worker's paradise, were inspiring. They seemed to spell doom for the hated czarist gov-ernment. And these ideas made it clear that rebellious youths like Stalin could lead this change.

For many, Marxism became a new religion. It replaced the Christian faith they had abandoned. Marx's writings became a kind of bible, through which the young revo-lutionaries sought to predict—and control—the future.

Years later, Stalin would say, "I joined the revolu-tionary movement at fifteen." Swept up in the revolu-tionary tide, he spent less and less time studying the religion he had rejected. He remained in school—perhaps out of fear of his mother—but became a rebellious student. He was sometimes punished by being forced to sit in a tiny cell for several hours.

These punishments did nothing to sway Joseph from the revolutionary path. He developed "a vicious, ferocious [hatred] against the school administration . . . against everything else that existed in the country and embodied Tsarism [Czarism]. Hatred against all authority."

During his time in Tiflis, Joseph read the *Revolutionary's Catechism*, a book written by a Russian revolutionary, Sergey Nachaev. The book spoke boldly of the violence required to bring about revolution : "Our task is terrible, universal destruction." According to Nachaev, revolutionaries must be prepared to kill and be killed to change the world order. They must be willing to commit horrible crimes to see the revolution through. Joseph took these lessons to heart.

By 1899 Joseph's rebellious behavior had made him an impossible student. He was expelled from the seminary that year, at the age of twenty-one.

Joseph in his twenties. Joseph spent much of this decade of his life living in poverty while working to bring Marxist revolution to the Russian Empire.

Chapter **TWO**

REVOLUTION

DISMISSAL **FROM THE SEMINARY BEGAN A LONG** period of uncertainty and movement for Joseph. For the next eighteen years, he spent much of his life as a wandering revolutionary.

Joseph traveled often, living an "underground" life. He used fake names and false identity papers. He was arrested seven times during this period. Although he spent some time in prison, he was mostly sentenced to exile in frozen Siberia. But exile was not very strictly enforced, and he usually escaped.

At some point during this period, Joseph became a member of a group of Marxist revolutionaries known as the Russian Social Democratic Labor Party (RSDLP). The RSDLP was led by a number of men who lived in exile outside of Russia. One of the group's leaders was a Russian-born revolutionary, Vladimir Ulyanov. Ulyanov would one day become famous under his revolutionary name—V. I. Lenin. Lenin and other RSDLP leaders called for the organization of protests and strikes throughout the Russian Empire. The RSDLP sent agents throughout the czar's territories to make this happen. The party also published an underground newspaper, called *Iskra* (the Spark). Its motto was "From the spark a flame [of revolution] will be kindled."

Joseph eventually became one of the party's top workers. He helped to organize worker strikes and demonstrations, wrote and published articles for *Iskra*, and engaged in expropriations—robbing banks and government agencies to pay for revolutionary activities. Joseph's hard work soon caught the attention of Lenin, who promoted him to a top-ranking position.

Although the RSDLP used the word *democratic* in its name, the party was anything but a democracy. All members were required to follow their leaders without question. Those who might question their leaders' actions, ideas, or interpretations of Marxism were condemned as enemies of the working class. Eventually, disputes about strategy and policy split the RSDLP into factions (rival groups within a party), with Lenin and Joseph becoming members of the Bolsheviks (majority men). Their main rival was the Mensheviks (minority men), who were led by a well-known revolutionary, Leon Trotsky.

STALIN

That same year, 1903, Joseph married Yekaterina (Kato) Svanidze, the daughter of a fellow Georgian revolutionary. Kato is described as very quiet and gentle and also very pretty. The newlyweds rented a tiny room near an oil field outside of Tiflis. Joseph did not have a job. Instead, he had to rely on handouts from revolutionary supporters, so the couple was extremely poor.

According to people who knew them, Joseph was occasionally violent toward his wife but also clearly fond of her. They did not have much of a normal home life. Joseph's revolutionary work often kept him away from home for long periods of time. In 1907 Kato gave birth to a son, Yakov.

Not long after Yakov's birth, Kato fell ill, probably with tuberculosis or typhus (infectious diseases that were common then). Her health quickly deteriorated, and Joseph, the penniless revolutionary, had no money for her treatment. In November 1907, she died—"in his arms," according to a family friend.

Joseph was devastated. After her funeral, he reportedly said, "This creature softened my stony heart. She is dead and with her have died my last warm feelings for all human beings." Yakov, just a few months old, was sent to live with his aunt and uncle.

By the early 1910s, Joseph had been publishing articles under a new revolutionary name—Stalin, or "man of steel." He had used numerous other false names. These included Koba, Ivanovich, K. Kato, and others. But

This arrest record from the early 1900s shows Stalin in his early thirties. Stalin was exiled to Siberia following the arrest.

apparently none of these names had the impact Joseph was looking for. Stalin demonstrated strength and power. It was in keeping with the last names of other high-ranking Bolshevik revolutionaries, such as Lev Kamenev (man of stone) and Vyacheslav Molotov (the hammer).

In March 1913, Stalin was arrested in Saint Petersburg. After spending several months in prison, the czarist authorities sent him into exile once again in remote Siberia, where temperatures often dropped to –46°F (–43°C). Stalin seemed destined to spend the rest of his life in poverty and obscurity. Then a series of events shook Europe to its foundations and brought the Russian Empire to its knees.

WORLD WAR I AND THE BOLSHEVIKS

During the summer of 1914, Europe was thrown into chaos. On June 28, the Austrian archduke, Franz Ferdinand, heir to the throne of the Austrian-Hungarian Empire, was assassinated. This act set in motion a complicated chain of events that led to World War I (1914–1918).

A complete set of agreements meant that Russia, France, and Great Britain (also known as the Allies) were thrust into a massive war against Germany and Austria-Hungary (the Central powers).

On the so-called Western Front of the war, Germany stood against France and Great Britain. On the Eastern Front, Russia faced off against Germany and Austria-Hungary. All armies on both sides suffered horrendous casualties (injuries and deaths) but made little progress toward victory.

Meanwhile, as the war raged on, Stalin remained in exile. He continued to write letters to acquaintances and fellow revolutionaries. He spent much of his time with a fellow Bolshevik exile, Kamenev.

By early 1917, the Russian public had lost patience with its government. In addition to the war's horrible cost in human life, the monetary cost of the war was also taking its toll. Food had become expensive and at times scarce. A bitterly cold winter had struck the capital, Petrograd (formerly and presently Saint Petersburg), making matters worse. By February 1917, resentment against the czar's government had reached a fever pitch.

THE FEBRUARY REVOLUTION

Late that month, rumors began that Petrograd would soon run out of bread. Panic gripped the city. Fearing starvation, crowds of citizens mobbed bakeries and shops, clearing the shelves.

Tens of thousands of citizens took to the streets to protest against the government. Shopkeepers shut down their shops, factory workers went on strike, students left their classes, even some government workers left their jobs to join the demonstration, chanting "Down with the czar!" "Down with the War!" and "Bread!"

These "bread riots" soon turned violent. Raging mobs swept through the streets looking to vent their anger. Policemen and soldiers were sent in to establish order. But the policemen were far outnumbered. And it soon became clear that many of the soldiers were on the side of the demonstrators.

In the days that followed, Petrograd became a war zone, as soldiers and policemen clashed with demonstrators. Dozens were killed. When the army troops assigned to protect the city refused to attack the demonstrators, the situation became a full-blown revolution. "It had now become clear to me," said one Russian official, "that we had lost all authority."

Czar Nicholas II and members of his family, above, *were taken prisoner following the bread riots of February 1917.*

Blood spilled onto the streets of Petrograd as the violence continued. Finally, Czar Nicholas II announced that he was abdicating, or giving up his rule. Nicholas and his family were taken prisoner.

News of these events spread throughout the country. It was soon announced that all political prisoners would be set free. Stalin and Kamenev boarded the first available train to Petrograd.

Stalin moved in with his friend Sergei Alliluyev and his family, including Alliluyev's two teenage daughters, Anna and Nadezhda (Nadya). Both of the young girls were in awe of the grizzled revolutionary living in their midst.

Stalin and Kamenev immediately went to work for *Pravda* (Truth), a successor to *Iskra*, which was declared a legal newspaper. Shortly after the czar's abdication, members of the Duma (the Russian legislature) created a provisional (temporary) government to rule the country. Writing in *Pravda*, Stalin and Kamenev both encouraged cooperation with the provisional government.

THE RETURN OF LENIN

When these issues of *Pravda* reached Lenin in Switzerland, he was furious. Only a full-scale Socialist revolution—led by himself and the Bolsheviks—would be acceptable.

The German government—hoping to see Russia give up its war effort—was happy to help Lenin in any way they could. They arranged for his safe passage through Germany to Russia. The Germans also gave Lenin vast sums of money to help him in his efforts to undermine the Russian government. "We had the idea," said one German general, "of using these Russians to speed up the demoralization of the Russian army."

Lenin arrived in Petrograd in early April. He immediately took charge of the situation. He condemned the provisional government and called for a true Socialist revolution to be headed by the only true Socialist party, the Bolsheviks.

Stalin, Kamenev, and the other Bolsheviks quickly fell in line behind their leader. Stalin once again demonstrated his reliability by writing and publishing dozens of articles for *Pravda* in support of Lenin's revolutionary views.

Later that month, the Bolsheviks held a party congress. They elected a new Central Committee, or group of top leaders. Stalin and Kamenev were among those selected. "We have known Comrade [Stalin] for many years," said Lenin. "He is a good worker in any responsible position."

Shortly after the congress, Lenin formed the Bureau of the Central Committee. This was an even smaller group of the top four Bolshevik leaders. Its members were Lenin, Lenin's right-hand man Grigory Zinoviev, Kamenev, and Stalin.

Lenin began to plot his Socialist revolution. He passed out the money he had received from the Germans to Bolshevik workers. He then sent them throughout Russia to spread the word of the new revolution. Lenin promised land for all of Russia's peasants. He promised to get Russia out of the war immediately. Hoping to create more mutinies in the armed forces, Bolshevik revolutionaries tried to convert army soldiers to the Socialist cause.

In May 1917, Menshevik leader Leon Trotsky returned to Russia. Although they had been bitter opponents, Lenin felt Trotsky would be useful to the party. He was popular and had a large following. Lenin convinced the charismatic Trotsky to join the Bolsheviks.

Over the next few months, party workers took control of local soviets (councils that had sprung up to deal with local affairs) throughout the country. By midsummer, Bolshevik membership had tripled from about 80,000 to 240,000.

Meanwhile, the provisional government was crumbling. Its members were in constant conflict and could do little to fix the country's many problems. Russia's citizens were losing patience.

THE OCTOBER REVOLUTION

"A Bolshevik rising is expected from day to day," wrote one Russian in October. On October 25, 1917 (according to the old Russian calendar, which was thirteen days behind the calendar used by most countries), the Bolsheviks seized the Winter Palace in Petrograd. The palace, a former residence of the czar, had been converted to the provisional government's meeting place. During the takeover of the palace, both Lenin and Stalin were hiding out several miles away. Stalin's key role was to help Lenin escape if the uprising failed.

After a standoff of several hours, the provisional government surrendered, and its members were taken prisoner. The Bolsheviks, a small, radical party with only a few hundred thousand members, had taken control of the largest country in the world.

A chaotic celebration followed. Bolshevik workers and soldiers raided the Winter Palace wine cellar, distributing thousands of bottles of wine and liquor to the crowds gathered outside. The partygoers soon turned into a vengeful, drunken mob. They wandered around the city, looting shops. Some people headed to

People flee fighting and death on the streets of Petrograd in October 1917. That month Bolshevik revolutionaries captured the Winter Palace and took control of the Russian government.

the wealthier parts of town and began robbing the nicer homes and killing their rich residents for sport.

Meanwhile, Stalin, Lenin, and the other weary Bolshevik leaders celebrated in a more subdued fashion. As they met to discuss what to do next, Lenin told Trotsky, "The transition from underground to power has been too sudden. My head is spinning."

This modern illustration shows Lenin, standing center, *Stalin,* right, *and other Bolshevik leaders planning the future of the Russian Communist state.*

Chapter **THREE**

CIVIL WAR AND TERROR

IN **FACT, AFTER YEARS OF WAR AND TWO VIOLENT** changes in government, the entire nation was spinning. The Bolshevik leaders knew they had much to do to build their Socialist state.

One of Lenin's first acts was to create a small policy-making body to control most government matters. This seven-man group, known as the Politburo, included Lenin, Stalin, and Trotsky. In endless meetings, Lenin, Stalin, and their colleagues tried to sort out how to build their new Socialist state. They wanted to abolish money and trade. Private property would become a thing of the past. At the new government's insistence, workers were taking control of factories. "Class warfare" began in earnest. The nation's poor class took revenge on the rich class. In many cases, factory owners were murdered by their former employees. Throughout the country, peasants seized the land of their rich landlords. Landlords who did not flee were often killed.

The Bolsheviks claimed these events were all part of the Marxist plan. Such policies were supposed to turn Russia into a Socialist state, then a Communist paradise. Yet according to Marx's theories, a true proletarian revolution would only be workable in an industrialized country. The leaders of the revolution would be factory workers. But Russia had very little industry. The vast majority of Russians were poor farmers. So in Marx's theory, Russia was not ready for Socialism.

Lenin chose to ignore this central part of Marxist theory. Instead, he resolved to force Russia into Socialism. Knowing that many of his policies would be unpopular, Lenin set out to destroy any opposition. Any ideas that spoke against the Bolsheviks were declared counterrevolutionary. Non-Bolshevik newspapers were shut down, and their print shops were destroyed.

Most importantly, Lenin established a secret police force, named the Cheka. This "Extraordinary Commission for Combating Counterrevolution and Sabotage by Officials" was declared the "punitive [punishing] sword of the Revolution." Cheka agents began a huge campaign to round up opponents to the regime. Those accused of counterrevolutionary activities faced imprisonment, torture, and often execution. Legal rights, such as the right to a fair trial, were abandoned. Many thousands of innocents were killed. The Russian people soon realized that their new government was far harsher than even czarist rule.

Each of the top Bolshevik leaders took posts in the new Soviet government. Stalin was appointed people's commissar for nationalities. He would deal with the many different countries and ethnic groups within the Russian Empire. In November 1917, Stalin and Lenin released a decree that included assurances that the non-Russian states of the former empire would have the right to become independent nations.

Meanwhile, the war continued. Germany was still eager to have Russia out of it. To put pressure on Lenin, the Germans launched an attack deep into Russia. By March 1918, a German army was approaching Petrograd. Lenin hastily moved the government to Moscow. Stalin went along. He took sixteen-year-old Nadya Alliluyev with him to work as his secretary.

Lenin was determined to make peace with the Germans at any cost. On March 3, the Bolsheviks signed a peace treaty that gave the Germans vast amounts of Russian territory and gold. But while Lenin had escaped from one war, another was just beginning.

THE REDS VS. THE WHITES

Throughout Russia people hostile to the Bolsheviks were forming armies to overthrow Lenin's regime, which had just renamed itself the Communist Party.

In southern and northwestern Russia, anti-Communists—provisional government supporters, czarist supporters, and others—gathered to fight against the Communists. The British and French, desperate to get Russia back into the war against Germany, also sent troops and military supplies. These forces—which came to be known as the Intervention—were soon joined by U.S., Italian, and Serbian troops. (The United States had entered the war on the side of France and Britain the year before.) In July Japanese troops fighting on the side of the Allies also landed in Vladivostok, in eastern Russia.

Threatened on all sides, Lenin placed the charismatic Trotsky in charge of the Communist armed forces. Marching under the red Communist Party flag, they were known as the Red Army. The anti-Communists were collectively known as the Whites. Major fighting began in the summer of 1918.

During the first years of the Russian Civil War (1918–1920), Stalin served in southern Russia. In June 1918, Lenin sent him to Tsaritsyn (modern-day Volgograd) to oversee Communist activities. Nadya Alliluyev once again went along to work as his secretary. At some point during the summer, sixteen-year-old Nadya and forty-year-old Stalin were married. Apparently, no ceremony took place. The two simply registered their marriage with the state. A few years later, Nadya gave birth to a son, Vasily.

Under a program called War Communism, Lenin

ordered that all surplus grain and other food products be handed over to the government to feed people in the cities. The peasantry bitterly opposed giving up their hard-earned goods. So War Communism had to be enforced by a brutal policy of "requisitioning." Stalin oversaw these actions in southern Russia. Food squads of party workers and Communist-friendly peasants roamed the countryside, seizing grain and shooting any who dared oppose them. The requisitioned grain was sent to the cities.

Such policies led even more Russians to join the Whites. In July a White offensive approached Tsaritsyn. Although Stalin had no military experience, Lenin placed him in charge of the defense of the city. But he refused to follow Trotsky's orders and was soon relieved of his duties and recalled to Moscow.

Meanwhile, Lenin feared that the White armies might rescue the former czar from imprisonment and use him as a rallying figure for their cause. So the Communist Party leader ordered the murder of Nicholas II and his entire family—including the czar's five children. The execution took place in July 1918.

Yet only weeks later, Lenin found himself on the wrong end of an assassin's gun. On August 18, a half-blind, mentally unstable woman shot him twice at point-blank range. Amazingly, his injuries were not life threatening. But the attempted assassination unleashed a spasm of violence across Russia.

On September 5, Trotsky announced a new offensive

against counterrevolutionaries." The result was the Red Terror. The Cheka stepped up its campaign against Bolshevik opponents, both real and imagined. "A campaign of mass murder developed throughout the country," writes Radzinsky. "People were swathed in barbed wire, eyes were gouged out, gloves were made of human skin, and people were impaled." Suspected counterrevolutionaries—the vast majority of them innocent of any antigovernment activities—were either executed or sent to prison camps, where they lived in awful conditions and performed slave labor for the state. Many of them were simply worked to death.

With no courts, no trials, no true rule of law, a simple accusation could lead to execution. Innocent people were tortured by Cheka agents until they "confessed." Citizens accused their neighbors, their friends—sometimes even their family members—of counterrevolutionary activities. People accused others to gain favor with the authorities or to save themselves from punishment. In many cases, an accused person's entire family was also imprisoned. Yet many of the accusers quickly found themselves accused in turn. "Terror was becoming a nationwide competition," writes Radzinsky.

The Red Terror and the war raged on throughout 1919. The Red Army, defending the central heartland of Russia, had an advantage over the Whites, who were scattered throughout the country. The Red Army was also a more unified force, brought together by the goal of Socialism and a merciless system of discipline.

A mother, right, mourns the loss of her sons, at her feet and to her right, who died fighting the White Army during the Russian Civil War. Both the Red and White armies suffered heavy losses, but victory went to the Reds.

Soldiers faced executions for even the slightest offenses. The Whites were equally brutal. But their makeup—many different groups with different goals and little mutual trust—made them less unified and therefore less effective.

By late 1920, the Communists had defeated the Whites. About eight hundred thousand soldiers had died in the civil war. Still, millions of Russians continued to resist Communist Party rule. Russia's suffering was nowhere near an end.

FAMINE

War Communism had devastated the countryside. Knowing that their grain would be taken, peasants had little incentive to work hard in their fields. A period of bad weather made the situation worse. By 1921 a massive famine was raging throughout the country.

Peasants carry two infants' coffins for burial during the Russian famine of 1921. The Communist government denied food relief to the starving, hoping to destroy the peasant economy.

With millions starving, Stalin served as on the government's Commission on Famine Relief. In reality, the commission's task was to deny help to the famine's victims. In particular, Stalin was charged with thwarting the American Relief Administration (ARA). This U.S. humanitarian organization helped save millions of Russians from starvation. The Communists regarded the U.S. efforts with contempt and suspected the Western capitalists might be trying to spread counterrevolution.

In fact, Lenin considered the famine useful. He "had the courage," said a fellow Communist, "to come out and say openly that famine would have numerous positive results. . . . Famine, explained [Lenin], in destroying the outdated peasant economy, would . . . usher in socialism."

Lenin, Stalin, and their fellow revolutionaries placed little value on human life. Nothing would stand in the way of their world revolution. As Nachaev had written in the *Revolutionary's Catechism*, "Our task is terrible, universal destruction."

Stalin did his best to harass the ARA. He even demanded that the Americans pay for the transportation of the food they were contributing to the country. The relief effort saved millions of lives, but still, about five million people died in the famine.

Communist policies were deeply unpopular, and public unrest continued. In March 1921, mass demonstrations against the Communists had taken place in the port of Kronstadt, in northern Russia. Trotsky sent in the Red Army to crush the demonstrators. But more such uprisings seemed imminent.

War Communism had failed. The public had refused to accept such hardships. So Lenin introduced a different system, called the New Economic Policy (NEP). NEP was a return to a limited form of capitalism. The Communists revived money, trade, and private property. Farmers and merchants were once again allowed to sell their goods. Russia was even allowed to sell and buy goods from its hated capitalist neighbors. NEP was a complete retreat from the revolution's aims. Some Communist leaders, including Trotsky, opposed the new concept. But the ever-loyal Stalin sided with Lenin.

Most historians believe that NEP was supposed to be a temporary measure to let the exhausted country recover from nearly a decade of war and hardship. But Lenin would never see the end of his program.

Lenin, left, *and Stalin,* right, *posed for this photograph in about 1921. While Lenin was the leader and public face of the Communist government, Stalin worked behind the scenes.*

Chapter **FOUR**

RISE TO POWER

THROUGHOUT THE REVOLUTION AND THE CIVIL WAR, Lenin and Trotsky had been the two best-known Communist figures. Stalin had stayed in the background. He was almost unknown to the general public. Yet behind the scenes, he had been accumulating a great deal of power.

As one of Lenin's most trusted aides, Stalin was given many important jobs. He had influence in the hiring of nearly every top government official. He also oversaw the hiring of most of the new government's lower-level workers. Stalin used his authority to fill government posts with Communists who were loyal to him.

In April 1922, Lev Kamenev proposed a new post— general secretary—to coordinate and oversee the many different arms of the Communist Party. Kamenev proposed Stalin for the post, and the rest of the Communist Party leadership quickly agreed.

The following month, Lenin suffered a severe stroke. He survived the episode but was left mentally weakened and physically impaired. His right side was paralyzed. Lenin was forced to deal with government issues by dictating letters or through visits to his home. On December 13, he suffered two more strokes.

Five days later, the Communist leadership placed Stalin in charge of Lenin's medical staff. Lenin's doctors ordered him to rest and take a break from political work. Stalin took it upon himself to enforce these orders. On December 22, he had a fateful confrontation with Lenin's wife, Nadezhda Krupskaya. When Stalin learned that Lenin had been writing to a colleague, Stalin telephoned Krupskaya and verbally abused her for allowing Lenin to disobey his doctors. Krupskaya was deeply offended.

LENIN'S TESTAMENT

That very day, Lenin suffered yet another stroke. It was becoming clearer to everyone—Lenin included—that the leader's failing health would prevent him from ever returning to his full-time duties. But who would succeed him?

Perhaps with this question in mind, the Soviet leader prepared what came to be called Lenin's Testament. Written in the form of a letter to the party's leadership,

Lenin summarized his opinions of the party's Central Committee members—Trotsky, Stalin, Kamenev, and others. The document was meant to be read to the Central Committee after Lenin's death.

Lenin's Testament described Trotsky and Stalin as "the two most able leaders of the present Central Committee." He expressed concerns about the personalities of both men. Stalin, "having become General Secretary, he has concentrated enormous power in his hands, and I am not sure that he always knows how to use that power with sufficient caution." Lenin went on to describe the other committee members in equally vague terms. The end result did little to clarify who should succeed Lenin.

On January 4, 1923, he added some other comments about Stalin. They showed a sudden change of mind:

> Stalin is too rude, and this defect, though quite tolerable in our midst and in dealings among us Communists, becomes intolerable in a General Secretary. This is why I suggest that the comrades think about a way to remove Stalin from that post and appoint another man who in all respects differs from Comrade Stalin.

Why did Lenin suddenly turn against Stalin? Was it because of the confrontation with Lenin's wife? Historians have presented this and other theories. It is also very likely that the other Central Committee leaders came to Lenin with concerns about Stalin. Kamenev, Trotsky, and others may have feared Stalin's post as general secretary gave him too much power. Lenin may also have resented Stalin's attempts to control Lenin through his doctors. "V.I. [Lenin] obviously got the impression," said Lenin's secretary, "that it was not the doctors who were advising the Central Committee, but the Central Committee giving instructions to the doctors."

In early March, Lenin finally confronted Stalin about his behavior toward Lenin's wife in the form of a forceful letter:

> Very respectable comrade Stalin,
> You allowed yourself to be so ill-mannered as to call my wife on the telephone and to abuse her. . . . I must ask you to consider whether you would be inclined to withdraw what you said and to apologize, or whether you prefer to break off relations between us.

Stalin's future in the party leadership was in jeopardy. He had no choice but to apologize. He was not about to admit he had made a mistake, however. He sent Lenin a letter that both apologized and denied any wrongdoing. He claimed he had not been rude to Krupskaya but apologized anyway "in order to preserve relations between us."

Meanwhile, the plot against Stalin was gathering

force. Lenin informed Trotsky and Kamenev that he was about to move "to crush Stalin politically." But on March 7, Lenin suffered yet another stroke. He lost his ability to speak, read, and write. The plot to crush Stalin never materialized.

In the years since, many have speculated that Stalin might have poisoned Lenin. Certainly the timing of the stroke was convenient for Stalin. But no evidence has ever emerged to support this idea. Most likely, the timing of Lenin's stroke was pure luck for Stalin. A recent medical study has suggested Lenin may have been suffering from syphilis, a sexually transmitted disease that affects the brain.

Lenin held on for several more months, but he no longer had any real political influence. The fight to replace him began in earnest.

In an abrupt change of fortune, Stalin found himself in a very strong position. As general secretary, he had the loyalty of the vast majority of Communist Party members. His chief rival was Trotsky. Trotsky was well known and had many supporters in the army and among party workers. Other candidates included Kamenev; Grigory Zinoviev, the top official in Petrograd; and Nikolay Bukharin, the editor of *Pravda*.

In the power struggle to come, Stalin held yet another important advantage. Most of his competitors had little understanding of how leadership and politics worked. Stalin, on the other hand, was a natural. He had a gift for manipulating events and using people to his advantage. In numerous cases, he simply outwitted his opponents.

Stalin also made use of a party rule that outlawed factions. Party members were allowed to debate a proposal until it became policy. But once a proposal was approved, all debate over it was outlawed. Lenin had suggested the policy a few years earlier to keep the party from splintering or even disintegrating into bickering factions. Stalin would use the rule to attain total power.

On January 21, 1924, Lenin died. Stalin organized an elaborate funeral ceremony. Lenin's body was embalmed and laid out in a coffin for public view. To strengthen

Lenin lies in state in 1924. Interestingly, Communist authorities removed Lenin's brain to study it. The organ remains in storage in the Soviet archives.

the public's connection between himself and Lenin, Stalin stood next to the casket as thousands of mourners filed past.

A few months later, Stalin delivered a series of lectures that highlighted Lenin's key philosophies, The Foundations of Leninism. They were soon published in a book under the same name that was widely read in Russia. The book promoted Stalin as the heir to Lenin and Leninism.

Stalin had Lenin's body carefully preserved. He placed it on permanent display in Moscow. He ordered a special shrine built so that the public could view the remains of their dead leader. In honor of Lenin, Petrograd was renamed Leningrad. In all of these actions, Stalin sought to create a "cult of personality." He portrayed Lenin as a near-perfect, almost godlike figure—with Stalin as his chief disciple.

Lenin's true feelings about Stalin were known only to a few insiders. In May 1924, Lenin's Testament was revealed to the party's Central Committee. But committee members shrugged off Lenin's warnings about Stalin, concluding that Lenin's illness had impaired his judgment. Furthermore, the committee ordered that the testament be kept secret. Once again, Stalin had dodged a bullet.

CRUSHING THE OPPOSITION

Throughout the rest of the 1920s, Stalin continued his rise toward supremacy. Even before Lenin's death,

Stalin had joined with Kamenev and Zinoviev to take on Trotsky.

Trotsky had long been opposed to NEP, which he felt was an unacceptable compromise to true Socialism. Trotsky called for a more Marxist policy dubbed Permanent Revolution. It was based on the Marxist theory that a Socialist revolution would have to be a worldwide event. A Socialist country could not succeed if it was surrounded by hostile capitalist neighbors, because capitalist governments would do everything in their power to destroy Socialism.

When they seized power, the Bolsheviks had expected the revolution to spread throughout Europe. But seven years after the Bolshevik takeover, the former Russian Empire—recently renamed the Union of Soviet Socialist Republics (USSR), or Soviet Union— remained the world's only Socialist country. The Bolsheviks had reversed their promises to the non-Russian countries of the old Russian Empire and refused to allow them true independence. Instead, Bolshevik-friendly leaders controlled the non-Russian countries. The Soviet Union was more or less an empire, just like the old Russian Empire.

In December 1924, Stalin introduced an alternative to the Permanent Revolution theory—Socialism in One Country. Stalin's concept stated that a Socialist state could survive and prosper within a capitalist world. Many party members saw it as a realistic alternative to Permanent Revolution.

Trotsky speaks to a crowd of followers in the 1920s. Stalin saw Trotsky as a stumbling block to his rise to power. A brilliant writer and electrifying public speaker, Trotsky was Stalin's chief rival for Lenin's position as Soviet leader.

But Trotsky and his supporters immediately attacked the idea, saying it was un-Marxist. Kamenev and Zinoviev viciously criticized Trotsky and his supporters, accusing them of defeatism. As a result of these quarrels, Trotsky's reputation, both within the party and among the general public, was permanently damaged.

Meanwhile, these party debates—at party meetings and congresses and covered in the press—led to resentment all around. The attacks on Trotsky had also lowered Kamenev's and Zinoviev's reputations. Stalin had cleverly remained in the background. He was seen as a voice of clearheadedness, unity, and moderation.

But Stalin was determined to eliminate all potential rivals. With Trotsky on the defensive, Stalin quickly turned on Kamenev and Zinoviev. He allied himself with Bukharin to attack his former comrades over issues relating to NEP. Bukharin, as the editor of *Pravda*, published article after article criticizing Kamenev and Zinoviev. The two responded with attacks of their own. At the Fourteenth Party Congress, in December 1925, Kamenev called for Stalin's removal. But party members shouted Kamenev down, instead cheering, "Long live Comrade Stalin!"

Thoroughly crushed, Kamenev and Zinoviev looked to Trotsky for help against Stalin. In mid-1926, the three were accused of violating the party ban on factions. In the months following, all three were removed from their positions of power.

HOME LIFE

During this time, Stalin and his wife Nadya lived in an apartment in the Kremlin in Moscow. This medieval fortress, with walls thirteen feet thick, housed most of the government's offices. Most Communist officials lived there. Stalin also had two *dachas*, or country residences. The couple sometimes stayed at these places on weekends or during brief vacations.

In 1926 Nadya gave birth to a second child. A girl, Svetlana, joined older brother Vasily. Yakov, Stalin's son by his first marriage, had come to live with them five years earlier.

Although Stalin appears to have genuinely loved his wife, their relationship was stormy. They often bickered and could rarely stand to be in the same room for long. They would go for days without talking to each other. Yet their letters to each other show a strong attachment. "I am kissing you passionately just as you kissed me when we were saying goodbye!" Nadya once wrote to her husband. Whatever the case, Stalin was rarely home. He often worked until late at night and came home only to go straight to bed.

Eyewitnesses described Nadya as selfish and moody. She probably suffered from severe depression. One of her family members described her as "sometimes crazed and oversensitive."

Stalin was often cruel and abusive to his sons, especially Yakov. Stalin detested Yakov's country bumpkin manner and his "gentleness and composure." In the early 1920s, when Yakov was eighteen, he married against Stalin's wishes. Stalin was furious and verbally abused his son. Yakov responded by attempting suicide. He tried to shoot himself, but the bullet only grazed his chest. When Stalin heard about the incident, he scoffed, "Ha! He couldn't even shoot straight!" Soon after, Yakov moved to Leningrad to live with Nadya's parents.

Stalin was less abusive toward Vasily, but his son still often bore the brunt of his bad temper. He was affectionate with his daughter Svetlana, however.

THE SHAKHTY TRIAL

As the tenth anniversary of the October Revolution approached, many Soviet citizens had begun to see the revolution as a failure. They had yet to see any reward for the sufferings of the civil war, War Communism, and famine. Although the country's economy had improved greatly under NEP, the living standard of the average Soviet citizen had not gotten much better. The Socialist/Communist paradise that the Bolsheviks had promised seemed anything but imminent. Meanwhile, some Soviet citizens had prospered and even become wealthy. Many hard-line Communists resented these newly rich folk. Stalin saw that this resentment could be used to strengthen his grip on power and to bring in the next stage of Socialism.

In early 1928, Stalin began to lay the groundwork for a new class war. He made a trip to Siberia, where he made speeches blaming the country's agricultural problems on greedy farmers. According to Stalin, these rich farmers, known as kulaks, were hoarding grain and refusing to sell it to the government. The kulaks were sabotaging Socialism.

Stalin also sowed the seeds for class warfare in the industrial sector. In early 1928, local party leaders in the coal mining area of Shakhty (in southwestern Russia) arrested fifty-three engineers and accused them of sabotage. The men were said to be "wrecking" the revolution by plotting to slow the production of coal. The "wreckers" were brought to Moscow and put on trial. The Shakhty Trial, as it came to be known, was a huge public spectacle that was covered by newspapers around the world.

The government had no evidence against the engineers, and the charges against them were surely false. But the secret police—following Stalin's orders—had picked them out as a means to ignite the new round of class warfare. They convinced some of the men— almost certainly via torture—to admit that they were guilty. In return, secret police agents promised to spare their lives.

Several of the engineers refused to confess, however, and the trial was quickly revealed as a sham. Early on at the trial, one man, Kolya Skorutto, at first proclaimed his innocence. The next day, he was absent. He returned to the courtroom the following day "an ash-grey trembling figure." Skorutto promptly confessed to his "crimes" and also accused his fellow wreckers. Skorutto's wife then shouted from the audience, "Kolya, darling, don't lie. Don't! You know you are innocent!" At that point, Skorutto burst into tears and withdrew his confession. He claimed he was confused and that he had not slept in eight days. (Sleep deprivation was a common secret police torture technique.) But by the next morning, Skorutto had again confessed.

Of the fifty-three defendants, eleven were sentenced to be executed (although six were eventually spared). Four were found not guilty, and four were given suspended sentences. The rest were imprisoned for from one to ten years.

Many observers realized the trials were a terrifying farce. U.S. reporter Eugene Lyons, who covered the trial, said it "left us limp with the impact of horrors half-glimpsed." But few Soviet leaders or citizens dared complain, for fear of becoming defendants themselves.

For Stalin the Shakhty Trial was a tremendous success. The spectacle had put the Soviet public on edge. It had shown that the battle for Socialism must be fought without mercy. "We have internal enemies," Stalin would say. "We have external enemies. This, comrades, must not be forgotten for a single moment."

Stalin used the Shakhty Trial as a model for future show trials. He would use them to constantly fan the fires of class warfare. Historian Robert Conquest describes the process:

> Once criminal charges were being investigated by the secret police, using methods no one in political circles was in a position to inquire into effectively, any attempt to pose such action at once took on the air of defending criminals and attacking the state and its investigative organs

Stalin was creating an atmosphere in which any questioning of the government—from government leaders or from the general public—could instantly be labeled as disloyal, counterrevolutionary, or treasonous. He was in the process of taking complete control of the country.

"HE WILL SLAUGHTER US ALL"

As the Shakhty Trial continued, Stalin was acting to eliminate the last of his competition—Bukharin and his allies. Bukharin favored NEP and believed that a gradual approach to Socialism was best. This position went against Stalin's drive for a new round of class warfare.

In February Stalin accused Bukharin and his allies of factionalism (dividing a group or government). Bukharin quickly came to the conclusion that Stalin was out to destroy him. In August 1928, he went to Kamenev seeking to form an alliance to bring Stalin down. "He is the new Genghis Khan," Bukharin said, comparing Stalin to the brutal Mongol ruler who had cut a swath of destruction across Asia and Europe in the twelfth and thirteenth centuries. "He will slaughter us all."

But the secret police quickly found out about the meeting. In November the Central Committee expelled Bukharin from the Politburo. His career was all but finished.

In February 1929, Stalin expelled Trotsky from the Soviet Union. (He would have him murdered a decade later.) Thus he had crushed the few men who had had any hope of challenging his power. Ruling over an empire of 142 million people, Stalin set out on a bold new plan to transform the Soviet Union from a backward, agricultural country into a modern, industrialized, Socialist state. The result would be one of history's greatest human tragedies.

Stalin in 1929, during the period of the first Five-Year Plan and the terror famine

Chapter **FIVE**

CLASS WARFARE

IN **APRIL 1929, S**TALIN **INTRODUCED THE FIRST**
Five-Year Plan. The scheme called for a massive crash
industrialization program. For example, the Five-Year
Plan ordered a stunning 180 percent increase in the
country's industrial production, a 335 percent increase
in electrical generation, and a swelling of the industrial labor force by 39 percent.

To pay for industrialization, the government expected
to purchase grain from the peasants and sell it over-
seas. But most peasants were reluctant to sell their
grain for the low prices the government offered.
Instead, they held on to it, hoping to sell it to private
grain traders for more money. Early on, it became
clear that the government would not be able to buy

enough grain from the farmers to finance its goals. So Stalin ordered government agents to the countryside to take grain—by force, if necessary. Thousands of activists and secret police agents fanned out across the nation. War Communism had returned, and like ten years earlier, many farmers resisted, often violently.

In part because of this resistance, Stalin called for the immediate mass collectivization of the countryside late in 1929. In Stalin's own words, collectivization meant "the transition from individual peasant farming to collective, socially conducted agriculture." In other words, the Soviet farmers would have to give up their

Women from a collective farm happily go on their way to work. The image is staged propaganda, designed to convince Soviets of the joys and benefits of the kolkhozy system.

individual plots of land. They would be required to work together with their neighbors in large collective farms, or kolkhozy. Each farmer's land, grain, tools, and livestock would become the property of the kolkhoz, which in turn was owned by the Soviet state. Thus the Soviet government would have control of virtually all the grain produced in the country.

Party workers sent out to enforce Stalin's orders were met with gunfire, riots, and mass protests. Stalin publicly blamed the kulaks for this resistance, although in reality farmers of all classes and incomes opposed collectivization.

Nevertheless, in early 1930, Stalin called for the "liquidation [disposal] of the kulaks as a class." A new terror swept across the countryside as neighbors accused neighbors of being kulaks. Over the next three years, nine to ten million alleged kulaks were either resettled on inferior land outside the kolkhozy, forced to move to other parts of the Soviet Union, or arrested and sent to prison camps in the outer regions of the country.

This war against the peasants devastated the country's agricultural sector. It stripped the countryside of many of its most productive farmers. Many peasants refused to give up their produce to the government. They destroyed or hid their grain and slaughtered their livestock. Farmers slaughtered about half of the nation's livestock in the first few years of the collectivization drive. Millions of peasants fled their farms

Young Communist Party workers forcefully confiscate a Soviet farmer's hidden grain from a cemetery during the famine years of the early 1930s.

to find work in the cities. Those who remained had little incentive to work, knowing most of their grain would be the property of the government. Stalin's policies crippled the Soviet Union's agricultural production. By 1932 the Soviet countryside was in the grip of another massive famine.

As the famine raged in late spring, the Soviet authorities demanded that peasants deliver to them millions of tons of grain from the upcoming harvest. In effect, the entire crop of a starving population was to be taken by the Soviet authorities.

To keep farmers from stealing grain to eat, guard towers were set up for "the protection of socialist property." Party workers swept through fields and homes, searching for hidden grain. People were executed or imprisoned for up to ten years for having just a handful of grain or food in their possession. Some starving peasants resorted to cannibalism to survive.

A Personal Tragedy

While famine laid waste to the countryside, life went on much as normal in the Soviet Union's urban areas. Although rumors of the famine reached Soviet cities, the state news sources said nothing about it. Instead, *Pravda* issued endless propaganda about the successes of collectivization, industrialization, and the Five-Year Plan. The government made propaganda films showing cheerful peasants living in luxury in the new kolkhozy.

Meanwhile, Stalin and his top men really did live in luxury in Moscow. "Despite the brutal war on the peasants . . . this time was a happy idyll [period]," writes historian Simon Sebag Montefiore, "a life of country weekends at peaceful dachas, cheerful dinners at the Kremlin, and languid warm holidays on the Black Sea." But privately, Stalin's relationship with Nadya was on edge again.

On the evening of November 8, 1932, Stalin and his wife attended a dinner party at the Kremlin. At the time, Nadya was probably suffering from a severe bout of depression. She may also have been struggling with the news she had heard from fellow students about the horrible famine raging in the countryside.

During dinner, Stalin and Nadya got into a spat. According to eyewitnesses, Nadya angered Stalin when she refused to raise her glass to Stalin's toast to "the destruction of the Enemies of the State" (the peasants or kulaks). When he asked her why she wouldn't drink, she ignored him. He responded by throwing orange peels and lit cigarettes at her.

As the evening wore on, the two continued to fight. Finally, Nadya left in a rage. Stalin remained at the party and did not return home that night.

The next morning, a member of the housekeeping staff found Nadya lying dead on the floor in a pool of blood, a small pistol by her side. She had left a suicide letter to Stalin.

Nadya's suicide devastated Stalin. The man who was at the same time delivering death to millions of peasants was shattered by grief. "She's crippled me," he said. "Oh Nadya, Nadya . . . how we needed you, me and the children."

He "was in a shambles, knocked sideways," said a colleague. But he soon recovered and began to see her suicide as a vicious betrayal. "She left me as an enemy," he said. After that, what remained of Stalin's family life more or less disappeared.

"WE'VE WON THE WAR"

The terror-famine lasted until spring of 1933. By then Stalin felt he had taught the peasants a lesson. Grain collection was halted in March of that year. Soon after, Soviet authorities began to release government stocks of grain to feed the starving peasants. "It took a famine to show them who is master here," said one party official. "It has cost millions of lives, but the collective farm system is here to stay. We've won the

SCENES FROM THE TERROR-FAMINE

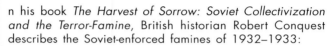

n his book *The Harvest of Sorrow: Soviet Collectivization and the Terror-Famine*, British historian Robert Conquest describes the Soviet-enforced famines of 1932–1933:

- In the towns, eerie scenes took place. People hurried about their affairs in normal fashion—and "there were starving children, old men, girls, crawling about them on all fours."

- A Ukrainian returning home from Siberia in 1933 found "the population in his village 'almost extinct.' His younger brother told him they were living on bark, grass and hares, but that when these gave out, 'Mother says we should eat her when she dies.'"

Meanwhile, party officials lived in comfort:

- "In [a] dining room [for public officials] at very low prices, white bread, meat, poultry, canned fruit and delicacies, wines and sweets were served to the district bosses."

war." Although exact numbers will never be known, seven to ten million people may have died as a result of collectivization and the terror-famine.

Meanwhile, the Soviet Union had, as planned, made significant strides toward industrialization. Thousands of factories had been built throughout the country.

Stalin had succeeded in bringing the backward Soviet economy into the modern world. But recent studies show that the collectivization effort had been so costly that it was little help in financing this achievement.

In January and February 1934, Stalin gathered the two thousand or so top Communist Party officials for the Seventeenth Party Congress. (The party had held congresses—meetings of top officials—on an irregular basis since 1898.) He named the 1934 gathering the Congress of the Victors. In his speech before the congress, Stalin boasted of the party's victories:

> There is no one to fight. . . . Everybody sees that the Party line is victorious, the policy of industrialization is victorious . . . the policy of liquidation of the kulaks, and total collectivization is victorious. . . . Our country's experience has shown that the victory of socialism in a single country is perfectly possible.

In speech after speech, party officials—including Stalin's former opponents—praised Stalin and his accomplishments. Bukharin called him "the personal embodiment of the mind and will of the party . . . its theoretical and practical leader." Kamenev said "This era . . . will go down in history . . . as the Stalin era."

But behind the gushing compliments, some of the older party leaders were once again looking for a way to cast Stalin aside. Having accomplished collectivization and

Stalin, left, and Sergey Kirov, right, in the early 1930s. After Nadya's suicide, Kirov became one of Stalin's closest friends and confidants. During this time, Kirov "cared for me like a child," Stalin once said.

industrialization, a bit of normalcy seemed to be returning to the country. Some party leaders wanted a new, less militant leader. Toward the end of the congress, one of Stalin's closest colleagues, Sergey Kirov, approached him with news that some party members had urged Kirov to run against Stalin in the election for general secretary. Kirov had refused the offer, but Stalin was furious.

A secret ballot had been scheduled for the end of the conference. The results of the election only added more fuel to his rage. Of the 1,225 delegates who voted, somewhere between 150 and 300 (the exact numbers are in dispute) voted against Stalin. He called the delegates who had voted against him "cowardly double-dealers." He soon began plotting a way to destroy not just the delegates who voted against him but virtually the entire party leadership. This included Kirov, even though Kirov had shown his loyalty by telling Stalin of the movement against him.

"WHAT A LAD!"

Meanwhile, a new leader had emerged in Germany. A year before the Congress of Victors, Adolf Hitler had been named chancellor of Germany. Over the next twenty months, Hitler and his Nazi Party would wipe out their political opponents to achieve total rule.

Although the Soviet leadership had been focused mostly on internal affairs, Stalin had closely followed Hitler's rise to power. On June 30, 1934, Hitler made one of his boldest moves. He ordered his most loyal followers to attack and kill many of his former allies. The Night of the Long Knives, as it came to be called, created an uproar in Europe. But Stalin was impressed

German chancellor Adolf Hitler, left center, *stands with members of the Hindenburg government in 1933. Public outcry forced German president Paul von Hindenburg,* right center, *to name Hitler to power that year.*

with Hitler's ruthlessness. "Hitler, what a lad!" he is quoted as saying. "Knows how to deal with political opponents."

But whatever Stalin's personal admiration for Hitler, Germany's Nazi Party and the Soviet Union's Communist Party were natural enemies. Hitler had destroyed the German Communists on his way to total power. He frequently expressed his contempt for Communism. The Soviet press responded in kind. It described Hitler's regime as evil and Fascist—referring to the violent and repressive political parties that had taken hold in several European nations after World War I.

Still, the two countries had much in common. They were both branded outcasts by the two other great European powers, France and Great Britain, and they were useful to each other. Germany wanted to rebuild its armed forces but was forbidden to do so under the terms of the Versailles Treaty, the agreement Germany had signed after losing World War I. Stalin would eventually allow the Germans to train in the Soviet Union. He wanted to use German military expertise to help build a modern army.

Hitler was perhaps most useful to Stalin because the threatening presence of Germany allowed Stalin to create a warlike atmosphere in the Soviet Union. In the early and mid-1930s, the Soviet press made much about the threat of the German warmongers. Stalin would use this threat to achieve total control of the Soviet government and population.

One of the last known photographs of Sergey Kirov, taken shortly before he was murdered in 1934

Chapter **SIX**

THE PURGES

ON THE EVENING OF DECEMBER 1, 1934, SERGEY Kirov was walking along a hallway to his office. Suddenly, a man stepped out from a darkened corner and shot him in the back with a pistol. Kirov died soon after, and the gunman, Leonid Nikolayev, was immediately taken prisoner.

Many historians believe that Stalin arranged to have Kirov murdered. Whether he did or not, Kirov's death benefited Stalin greatly. The act got rid of one of Stalin's potential rivals. But more importantly, the murder provided Stalin with yet another excuse to deal with his potential enemies.

Just hours after hearing the news of Kirov's death, Stalin issued a decree calling for a new and ruthless

THE STALINISCHINYA AND THE TWENTY MILLION

P eople in the former Soviet Union refer to the time of Stalin's rule as the Stalinischinya. They often speak of Stalin's victims as simply "the twenty million." Virtually every person who lived during that time (from about 1929, when Stalin defeated his main rivals and grasped supreme control over the Soviet Union, to 1953) knew or knew of someone who was a victim of Stalin's rule. All lived in fear of winding up victims themselves.

About one-third to one-half of these people died in the government-enforced famine of the early 1930s. The rest perished in interrogation chambers, execution rooms, or in or on their way to the gulag—the vast system of Soviet prison camps.

It is difficult to grasp such a huge number as twenty million. In an attempt to put this "statistic"—as Stalin would have called it—into perspective, think of each word of this twenty-thousand-or-so word book as representing one thousand deaths. This sentence you are reading represents eleven thousand of Stalin's victims.

"procedure to be followed in dealing with terrorist acts against officials of the Soviet regime." Investigation of all such cases was to be finished in no more than ten days. Most cases would not be tried in public. All those convicted were to be sentenced to death and executed immediately. This sweeping order gave Stalin the power to unleash a new wave of terror in the Soviet Union.

In public Stalin expressed shock and grief at Kirov's death. At the funeral, Stalin's "face was sorrowful," according to one eyewitness. Seemingly overwhelmed with grief, he even bent over his fallen comrade's coffin and kissed him on the forehead!

Nikolayev, Kirov's assassin, was executed within weeks of the Kirov murder and the only witness to the shooting, Kirov's bodyguard, died in a mysterious car accident. Soviet secret police soon arrested Zinoviev, Kamenev, and many of their followers. All were blamed for Kirov's murder. The Soviet government

Stalin, right front, *helps carry Kirov's coffin to its burial site in the Kremlin wall.*

accused them of hatching a plot to kill Stalin and other top Soviet officials. Zinoviev's and Kamenev's followers were quickly tried and executed. But Stalin had other plans for his old friends.

Stalin and the secret police persuaded Zinoviev and Kamenev to accept "moral responsibility" for Kirov's murder. In essence, they agreed to say that their earlier opposition to the party's plans had inspired the murder of Kirov. In return for their confessions, the two men probably expected to be pardoned. Instead, Zinoviev was sentenced to ten years in prison, Kamenev to five years.

But these convictions were only the beginning. In the coming months, the Soviet press reported details of a widespread conspiracy infecting the Soviet Union. *Pravda* informed the public that Trotsky (who was still in exile), Kamenev, and Zinoviev had set up terrorist groups throughout the country.

Over the next four years, millions of Soviet citizens were arrested and accused of terrorist activities. Although virtually none of them were guilty of any crimes, the vast majority of these "enemies of the people" were tortured until they confessed. They were then convicted and executed or sent to the gulag—the country's system of slave labor camps, mostly in Siberia. Stalin directly oversaw much of this great purge. One estimate states that he personally signed execution orders for 230,000 people during this period.

New Show Trials

Meanwhile, Stalin kept the country in a state of panic by holding several show trials during the mid-1930s. The first trial took place in August 1936. He pulled Zinoviev and Kamenev out of prison in order to use them as defendants in one of the trials. Fourteen others were also accused of creating a terrorist network with the help of Trotsky. All confessed and were executed the day after the trial ended.

A second trial took place in January 1937. The Soviet government accused twenty-one top Soviet officials of working with the exiled Trotsky to sabotage the Soviet economy. They were also accused of working with Germany and Japan to help overthrow the

Grigory Zinoviev in the 1930s. Zinoviev, Stalin's former ally, was forced to testify that he had contributed to Kirov's murder. He was sentenced to ten years in the gulag. Zinoviev later testified against others—in hopes of avoiding a firing squad—but he was executed in 1936.

Soviet government. All the defendants were found guilty. Nineteen were executed. Two were sentenced to ten years in prison.

Stalin held the third major show trial a little over a year later. Among the twenty-one defendants was Stalin's old friend Bukharin. Another was Genrikh Yagoda, the former head of the secret police. Yagoda had most likely played a key role in Kirov's murder. And as head of the secret police, the cold-blooded Yagoda had overseen the torture and execution of hundreds of thousands of "enemies of the people." But by this time, Yagoda was more useful to Stalin dead than alive. He and the rest of the defendants were convicted. Yagoda, Bukharin, and sixteen of the other defendants were executed.

In the end, Stalin succeeded in destroying not only any potential enemies but virtually the entire old Soviet leadership. He purged nearly every top official who had been involved in the Bolshevik overthrow of the czar and the civil war. Among the 1,225 voting delegates from the 1934 Congress of the Victors, 1,108 were arrested. Most were either executed or sent to the gulag.

These purges destroyed any threat of opposition to Stalin's leadership and also all independent thought in the Soviet Union. Virtually the entire Soviet population dared speak nothing but praise for their ruler. This system of total control over the entire population is known as totalitarianism. Soviet writer Isaac Babel (who would himself be executed at the beginning of the next decade) described the atmosphere of these times:

"Today, a man only talks freely with his wife, at night, with the blankets pulled over his head."

During this same period, Stalin hunted down potential enemies in the Soviet Union's armed forces. In May 1937, the Soviet press announced that the secret police had arrested several high-ranking military leaders, including the country's top military leader, Marshal Mikhail Tukhachevsky.

Tukhachevsky was a hero of the civil war. But Stalin saw the handsome and popular Tukhachevsky as a potential rival. The marshal and many of his fellow officers confessed to being involved in terrorist conspiracies after being tortured by agents of the secret police. Tukhachevsky's interrogation record was stained with blood, probably his own.

Over the next few years, about forty thousand military officers and soldiers were arrested. Nearly fifteen thousand were executed. The rest were sent to the gulag. By the end of the decade, Stalin had wiped out all potential rivals from the Soviet military. But he had bled his military of nearly all of its experienced officers. To take their places, Stalin assigned his own loyal but inexperienced—and often incompetent—followers. Meanwhile, Europe was bracing for war.

HITLER ON THE MARCH

By the mid-1930s, Hitler was openly defying the Versailles Treaty. Germany's well-trained and well-armed forces were on the move in Europe.

In early 1938, Hitler began a series of bold moves to expand German-controlled territory. Germany first annexed (took over) Austria. Later, Hitler annexed Czechoslovakia (the modern-day Czech Republic and Slovakia). The German leader's next move would probably be to invade Poland. Such a move would put the German army at the Soviet Union's doorstep.

France and Great Britain had done little to stop Hitler. But in 1939, the British and French announced that they would declare war on Germany if it invaded Poland. Hitler's actions had left Stalin with a grim choice. War was coming, and he would probably not be able to stay out of it. He had to choose sides. The Soviet Union was the sworn enemy of both the anti-Communist Hitler and the capitalist French and British.

In public Stalin declared his contempt for both sides, saying that Soviet policy would "not allow our country to be drawn into conflicts by warmongers." But in secret, Stalin was looking to strike a deal.

Some Western leaders felt that a French-British-Soviet military alliance might be enough to discourage Hitler. But the Western powers dragged their feet in negotiations and offered Stalin little incentive to join them. An alliance with the West would probably mean fighting Germany very soon. Having purged his armed forces of its leadership, Stalin probably did not think his country was ready for a major war.

On the other hand, Germany proposed a much better deal. On August 23, 1939, Stalin and Hitler agreed to the Molotov-Ribbentrop Pact (named after the foreign ministers of the Soviet Union and Germany, respectively). For promises not to fight each other, the two countries agreed to divide Eastern Europe between them. Hitler granted Stalin control of eastern Poland, Finland, Latvia, Lithuania, and Estonia.

At the celebration following the signing of the pact, Stalin proposed a toast to Hitler. "I know how much the German people love its Führer [leader]. I would therefore like to drink to his health."

Announcement of the pact shocked the West. Nothing stood in the way of a new European war.

On September 1, 1939, German forces invaded Poland. Hitler's army and air force smashed their way deep into Polish territory. The new German tactic of blitzkrieg (lightning war) quickly overwhelmed the Poles and stunned the rest of Europe. As promised, France and Britain immediately declared war on Germany. World War II (1939–1945) had begun.

By September 9, German forces had captured the Polish capital of Warsaw. Eight days later, Red Army troops invaded from the east. (France and Britain did little to help the Poles.) Poland was doomed. Within weeks, German and Soviet troops had conquered the entire country.

Meanwhile, Hitler's blitzkrieg stampeded across Europe. Norway, Denmark, Belgium, and the Netherlands all fell to German forces. Stalin helped to fuel Germany's war machine by selling them huge amounts of oil, grain, cotton, and other materials at good prices.

In the early summer of 1940, Hitler's forces routed French and British troops stationed in France. By mid-June, France belonged to Hitler. Only Great Britain stood in the way of Hitler's complete dominance of western Europe. Battered and weakened, the British had few resources for taking the fight to Hitler at the end of the summer of 1940.

Hitler's successes left Stalin in a dangerous position. He had counted on the Western powers and Germany to fight it out, perhaps leaving him to finish off the weakened survivor. Instead, Hitler stood as master of much of Europe. The only countries powerful enough to challenge him were the United States (which had up to this point stayed out of the fighting) and the Soviet Union.

But Hitler was not content with controlling western Europe. He soon began making plans to conquer the Soviet Union. In December he signed the orders authorizing Operation Barbarossa—the invasion of the Soviet Union—to begin in the spring of 1941.

During the early months of 1941, Stalin received numerous reports that a German attack was imminent. German troops were massing on the eastern border of German-controlled Poland. One report even listed the date of the invasion, June 22, 1941. Stalin responded to these reports with anger and disbelief. He accused the agents of lying and trying to provoke a war. Few of Stalin's top men dared even suggest that

German soldiers and military vehicles pour across the Soviet Union's western border in 1941. Hitler's blitzkrieg had come to Stalin and the Soviet Union.

war could be on the horizon. Stalin's system of unquestioning obedience did not allow for open-minded discussion. Meanwhile, the Soviet public had heard nothing but praise for Germany since the signing of the Molotov-Ribbentrop Pact. They had been told that war was not possible.

Still German troops continued to gather on the Soviet Union's western borders, while German reconnaissance (scout) planes flew into and out of Soviet territory. On the night of June 21, 1941, Stalin said to his top military leader, Marshal Georgy Zhukov, "I think Hitler is trying to provoke us. He surely hasn't decided to make war?" Hours later, three million German troops, thirty-six hundred German tanks, and twenty-five hundred German aircraft answered his question.

German soldiers display a broken bust of Stalin they destroyed during the 1941 German offensive in the Soviet Union. Like the bust, Stalin himself fell apart for a few days at news of the German invasion.

Chapter **SEVEN**

THE GREAT PATRIOTIC WAR

BY JUNE 28, 1941, THE GERMANS HAD PUSHED three hundred miles into Soviet territory. The German blitzkrieg had encircled four hundred thousand Red Army troops and taken the city of Minsk (in modern-day Belarus). As the full scale of the disaster became clearer and clearer, Stalin became unhinged.

"Everything's lost," Stalin is said to have declared. "I give up. Lenin founded our state and we've [messed] it up." He announced that he was resigning and went home to his dacha.

For two days, Stalin sulked at home while the Soviet government was left in chaos. According to Molotov, he "had shut himself away from everybody, was receiving nobody and was not answering the phone." No one knew what to do. Stalin's top men—Molotov, Zhukov, and others—did not dare to issue orders without Stalin's permission. When—or if—Stalin returned, they might be punished for trying to steal their leader's authority. Meanwhile, the Germans were rolling eastward, leaving destruction in their wake.

On June 30, Molotov, Beria, and a few others went to the dacha to try to convince Stalin to come back to work. When they arrived, they found their leader sitting in an armchair, looking "gloomy."

"Why've you come?" he asked worriedly. He probably expected them to arrest him. Molotov said, "We're asking you to come back to work." They asked Stalin to take control of the fight against Germany. Stalin accepted.

"I Call upon You, My Friends"

Stalin finally spoke to the Soviet public on July 3. "Brothers and sisters!" he began. "Warriors of the army and the fleet! I call upon you, my friends." The man who had for the last two decades waged war against his own people, executing and imprisoning millions, was calling on his "brothers," "sisters," and "friends" to rally behind him to defend the motherland in what came to be known as the Great Patriotic War.

But calls for unity did little to stop the advancing Germans. By mid-July, the Soviets had lost about two million soldiers, thirty-five hundred tanks, and six thousand aircraft. The Red Army was in tatters. During the early months of the war, Stalin had insisted on having control of military matters. His lack of military training and unwillingness to listen to his commanders resulted in numerous defeats and hundreds of thousands of deaths.

Given the harshness of Stalin's rule, it is not surprising that some Soviet citizens welcomed the Germans as liberators. But Hitler's forces quickly showed themselves to be just as brutal as the Soviets, destroying homes and villages and massacring civilians. The Soviet people were thus caught in a struggle between two horrifying powers.

As the summer wore on, Hitler's forces tore across the western Soviet Union. By autumn, a massive German army had surrounded Leningrad, while another was approaching the suburbs of Moscow.

All seemed lost. But before the Germans could make their knockout blow on Moscow, winter set in. The cold and snow made a major attack impossible. The brief break finally gave the Red Army time to regroup and prepare to fight. The Germans lacked warm winter clothes, because Hitler had expected to conquer the Soviet Union before winter. Their machines did not operate well in the harsh Russian climate.

Stalin put Zhukov, a brilliant military leader, in charge of the defense of Moscow. On December 5, 1941, Zhukov staged a massive counterattack to push the Germans away from the capital.

The battle for Moscow lasted three months. Finally, the Red Army pushed the Germans back. Almost one million soldiers from both sides were killed. For the first time since the war began, the Germans had been beaten.

ALLIES

By the spring of 1942, the outlook for Stalin and the Soviet Union was improving. Months earlier, the Japanese had attacked the U.S. naval base at Pearl Harbor in the Hawaiian Islands. The attack brought the United States into the war against Japan and Germany. Already Britain and the United States were making plans to open a new front in the war against Hitler.

Soviet soldiers return fire on German forces from the rubble of a bombed-out building during the Battle for Stalingrad (1942–1943).

Relations between the new allies were far from smooth. Desperate for some relief against the Germans, Stalin never missed a chance to demand that the United States and Great Britain do more to help him. Both countries helped the Soviets with massive amounts of war supplies. Still Stalin remained ungrateful. The Russians "despise us and have no use for us except for what they can get out of us," complained a British military leader.

In 1942 Soviet forces defeated the Germans in a vicious struggle for the industrial city of Stalingrad (modern-day Volgograd). About two million died on both sides of the battle—more than half of them Soviet soldiers and citizens.

The next year, the Red Army and Air Force won another epic battle. At Kursk in western Russia, about two million soldiers, six thousand tanks, and four thousand aircraft slugged it out over a period of six weeks in the largest battle in history. The Soviet victory at Kursk greatly weakened the Germany army. From then on, Stalin's forces would be on the offensive.

Over the next two years, the Red Army fought its way westward against a crumbling German army. In 1944 Soviet troops drove the Germans out of the Soviet Union and then rolled into Poland, Romania, Bulgaria, and Yugoslavia, present-day Serbia, Bosnia, and Montenegro.

For many of the people living in the formerly German-occupied areas, the Soviet liberation would prove to be anything but liberating. Stalin's secret police arrested millions of citizens on the suspicion that they had been tainted by the German occupation. Hundreds of thousands of members of ethnic groups from the German occupied areas of southwestern Russia, including the Chechens, the Kalmyks, and the Karachai, were rounded up by armies of secret police and deported by train to the gulag. About a third of these people—perhaps as many as six hundred thousand or more—died en route.

As the Red Army swept into the non-Soviet countries, Stalin was coming into conflict with his allies. British prime minister Winston Churchill and U.S. president Franklin Delano Roosevelt had expected Stalin to allow these countries to form their own democratic governments. But once the Red Army occupied Poland, Romania, and Bulgaria, Stalin began to install governments led by loyal Communists. Democracy would not be in the cards for the citizens of these countries. Instead, they would live under Stalinist governments for many decades to come.

At a conference between the three leaders in Yalta (in southern Ukraine) in February 1945, Roosevelt and Churchill protested against Stalin's actions in Eastern Europe. But there was little they could do to stop him. The Red Army had grown to 13.5 million strong —by far the largest army ever. After years of fighting the most costly war in history, the thought of the United States and Britain taking on the mighty Soviet Union was out of the question.

Victorious Soviet forces raise the Soviet flag over the Reichstag (parliament building) in Berlin after capturing the German capital city in May 1945.

Victory

By spring of 1945, Soviet troops were well inside Germany and on their way to the capital, Berlin. With the war lost, Hitler committed suicide on April 30. On May 8, Germany surrendered. The war in Europe was over, though it still raged in Asia. The Soviet people had won the Great Patriotic War but at a horrendous cost. Although exact numbers are unknown, many historians estimate that about twenty-seven million Soviet people died as a result of the war. Another twenty-five million were left homeless.

But for Soviet soldiers who had been unlucky enough to be captured by the Germans, the suffering was far from over. Stalin believed that these men and women had been tainted or corrupted during their time in prison camps. So secret police shipped many of the prisoners straight from German prison camps to the gulag.

In July 1945, Stalin met with British and U.S. leaders at Potsdam, Germany. The new British prime minister, Clement Attlee, and the new U.S. president, Harry S. Truman, once again criticized Stalin's setting up of "puppet" governments in Eastern Europe, but there was little they could do. The balance of power was clearly in Stalin's favor. Yet at the conference,

Stalin, back center in white, *negotiates the fate of Germany and Eastern Europe during the 1945 Potsdam Conference. U.S. president Harry S. Truman is at the far right, facing the camera.*

Truman casually mentioned that the United States had just successfully tested a new superweapon that might tip the scales the other way.

Stalin, through his spies, already knew about the weapon—the atomic bomb. The following month, the rest of the world learned the secret when U.S. aircraft dropped atomic bombs on the Japanese cities of Hiroshima and Nagasaki. The bomb blasts were like nothing ever seen before. They leveled both cities with massive fireballs, killing tens of thousands. The Japanese soon surrendered, ending World War II.

Stalin had already approved a massive research program to develop a Soviet atomic bomb. He placed Lavrenty Beria, his most ruthless assistant, in charge.

Meanwhile, the disputes that had been brewing between Stalin and his allies were only beginning. Nearly all of Eastern Europe, including much of eastern Germany, was firmly under Stalin's control. The world was becoming divided between Stalin's Communist-controlled states of Eastern Europe and the democratic nations of the West. Former British prime minister Winston Churchill summed up the situation in a speech in the United States in March 1946, when he said, "An iron curtain has descended across the continent [of Europe]."

A new kind of war was brewing, a war in which nearly every nation in the world would be forced to take sides. This war—the Cold War (1945–1991)—would impact world events for an entire generation.

Stalin in the late 1940s. The stress of the years of brutal rule had taken its toll on his physical and mental health.

Chapter EIGHT

THE COLD WAR

IN MY OPINION," WROTE NIKITA KHRUSHCHEV, "IT was during the war that Stalin started to be not quite right in the head." By the late 1940s, as Stalin approached the age of seventy, his physical and mental health had begun to decline. He suffered a minor stroke after the end of the war and spent several months recuperating. His lifelong habit of smoking cigarettes and pipes added to his troubles. In the last years of his life, Stalin suffered from rheumatism (painful inflammation of the muscles and joints), high blood pressure, giddy spells, dizzy spells, and arteriosclerosis (hardening of the arteries). He had lost most of his teeth. "Cursed old age has arrived," he complained to his associates.

TOTALITARIAN FICTION: *DARKNESS AT NOON, 1984,* AND *ANIMAL FARM*

Three popular novels of the mid-twentieth century bring to life the horrors of totalitarianism. *Darkness at Noon* (1940), written by Hungarian-born former Communist Arthur Koestler, follows the story of Rubashov, a high-ranking former revolutionary who is arrested by the secret police of a fictional government that was clearly modeled on the Soviet Union. Under interrogation, Rubashov is forced to look back at his past and the crimes committed by his government for the sake of Communism. The novel captures the fear and madness that gripped the Soviet Union during the purges of the 1930s.

In *1984* (1949) British author George Orwell creates a futuristic totalitarian society, where a corrupt and deceitful government keeps watch on all of its citizens at all times and all independent thought is considered a crime. Orwell also wrote *Animal Farm* (1945), a kind of fable, written with clear parallels to the Russian Revolution and Stalin's totalitarian state. In it a group of barnyard animals overthrow their cruel human masters and create a new society, where all the animals are supposedly equal. But eventually the smartest and most power-hungry animals, the pigs, seize control of the farm and create a society far more cruel than the one they had overthrown.

But Stalin's grip on the Soviet people—and by this time, also, the people of Eastern Europe—was tightening again. After all the hardships of the war, many Soviet citizens had hoped for a new era of peace, prosperity, and freedom from fear. But as always, Stalin believed he needed enemies, fear, and terror to maintain his stranglehold on the Soviet people.

Churchill's "Iron Curtain" speech provided Stalin with an outside threat. Throughout the late 1940s, *Pravda* and the Soviet news service TASS (Telegraph Agency of the Soviet Union) issued an endless stream of propaganda about the West, falsely describing the horrible life of people living under capitalism. In one case, the Soviet media described the machine-gunning of innocent workers in London, when no such event actually occurred.

Shortly before the end of the war, Stalin is reported to have said, "The war will soon be over. We shall recover in fifteen or twenty years, and then we'll have another go at it." He would never dare start another war as long as the United States had the advantage of the atomic bomb. But months before the 1940s ended, the Soviets successfully tested their own atomic bomb. Soon his scientists had developed even more powerful nuclear weapons.

In Stalin's mind, he was almost ready for a showdown with the West. Armed with nuclear weapons, the largest army in history, and a thoroughly obedient population, he held a tremendous military advantage over the West. Recent Russian research suggests that Stalin may in fact have been setting the stage for a World War III, in which he expected that Communism would destroy capitalism once and for all, bringing to reality the "dream" of a Communist world. Said Stalin to Molotov, "The First World War delivered one country from capitalist slavery, the Second has created the socialist system [meaning the Soviet domination of Eastern Europe], and the Third will finish imperialism forever."

THE DOCTOR'S PLOT

Meanwhile, inside the Soviet Union, Stalin was laying plans for a new wave of terror. In 1948 Jews throughout the world celebrated the birth of the State of Israel. This homeland for the Jewish people was founded in the wake of the Holocaust. During the Holocaust, Hitler and his henchmen had murdered about six million Jews in a plan to wipe out the European Jewish population.

In the autumn of 1948, Golda Meir arrived in the Soviet Union as the Israeli ambassador. Crowds of Soviet Jews poured into the streets to welcome her. For Stalin, such affection for a foreigner was unacceptable. Soviet citizens could be loyal only to the Soviet Union, only toward Stalin himself. In anti-Semitism (hostility toward or discrimination against Jews), Stalin found a source for a fresh round of terror.

Soon after Meir's arrival, *Pravda* and TASS began to publish a steady stream of anti-Semitic propaganda. Citizens were encouraged to report suspicious activity by Jews, and many Jews were arrested, tortured, and imprisoned. By the early 1950s, Stalin's anti-Semitic campaign was in high gear—Jews were fired from their jobs and even beaten up on the streets.

By early 1953, the Soviet authorities were busy setting up camps in the outer reaches of the Soviet Union.

Millions of Soviet Jews were to be rounded up and sent to these slave labor prisons. To mobilize the Soviet people for his anti-Jewish campaign, Stalin was assembling a cast for a new run of show trials. TASS and *Pravda* reported the uncovering of a sinister "Doctor's Plot" to assassinate the country's top political leaders, including Stalin himself.

The secret police arrested several prominent Jewish doctors. Among them was Dr. V. N. Vinogradov, Stalin's own personal physician. Vinogradov had made the mistake of telling the aging Stalin that he should spend more time resting. Stalin interpreted this as an attempt to move him out of power.

The show trials were set to begin in the summer of 1953. As had happened in the past, the accused would confess to their fictional crimes and be hanged in Red Square in Moscow. The trials would bring anti-Semitism to a fever pitch in the Soviet Union. Millions of Soviet Jews would be deported to the country's wastelands.

Once again, Stalin was mobilizing his country through terror. Some historians even believe that Stalin had planned his attack on the Soviet Jews to draw protest from the West—that he hoped to bait the capitalist countries into war. The elimination of the Soviet Jews would be the first steps on the road to a nuclear World War III. This war would bring about the destruction of capitalism and the birth of a Communist world, with Stalin as supreme ruler. But these plans expired with Stalin's last breath on the night of March 5, 1953.

EPILOGUE

Stalin's sudden death sent a wave of grief across the Soviet Union. The crowds at his funeral swelled to such numbers that many people were crushed to death. Given the shocking crimes of his rule, this reaction is difficult to understand. But for decades, the Soviet people had been fed endless propaganda about Stalin—his strength, his wisdom, his kindness, his determination to destroy all enemies of Communism. As Soviet nuclear scientist Andrey Sakharov said: "It was years before I fully understood the

Mourners attend Stalin's funeral in 1953. His body would lie in state alongside Lenin's until 1964, when it was removed in recognition of Stalin's crimes against the Soviet people.

degree to which deceit, exploitation and outright fraud were inherent in the whole Stalinist system. That shows the hypnotic power of mass ideology."

Stalin's preserved body was displayed next to Lenin's in Moscow. Within a few years, Nikita Khrushchev would emerge as the head of the government.

Shortly after Stalin's death, Soviet authorities released about seven or eight million political prisoners. The Soviet Union's new leadership was less brutal than Stalin's—no mass terrors would ever occur in the Soviet Union again—but the Communist Party had no intention of giving the Soviet people true freedom and democracy. The Cold War continued, TASS and *Pravda* remained under the control of the government, and the secret police maintained its grip on the population.

In 1956 Khrushchev made a four-hour "secret speech" to the country's top Communist officials. In it he described and condemned the crimes of Stalin and Stalinism. Khrushchev's speech was the beginning of a slow, unsteady process of facing up to the horrors of Stalin's rule. Although free from Stalin's deadly grip, the people of the Soviet Union and Eastern Europe continued to suffer under Communism. For all but the top officials, life was bleak. Citizens lived in run-down, crowded apartments and had access to few consumer goods. Most still lived in fear of being arrested for no reason. Only the most courageous people dared voice their political views. All lived under the watchful eye of the secret police.

Throughout the 1960s, and 1970s, the Cold War dragged on. As the United States and the Soviet Union spent billions of dollars developing more powerful nuclear weapons and better ways to deliver them, the entire world lived in fear of a massive nuclear showdown between East and West. But by the 1980s, Communism was crumbling. In large part due to the arms race, the Soviet Union was going bankrupt.

In the early 1980s, a new Soviet leader, Mikhail Gorbachev, called for changes in the Soviet Union. Hoping to find a way to solve the country's problems, he encouraged *glasnost*, or openness. For the first time, Soviet citizens were given the freedom to talk about the country's troubles and the crimes of the past, especially the crimes of the Stalin era.

But glasnost did not solve the Soviet Union's problems. Instead, Soviet citizens seized their new freedoms and demanded more. In the late 1980s, the Soviet-dominated countries of Eastern Europe declared their independence from Moscow. At the same time, the nations of the Soviet Union demanded the right of self-rule. As historian Martin Amis put it, "Glasnost . . . laughed the Bolsheviks off the stage." On December 25, 1991, the Soviet Union, which had promised to bring a worker's paradise to earth and had brought about tens of millions of deaths in the pursuit of this dream, ceased to exist. But the horrors of Stalin's crimes live on in the memories of his victims and in the many accounts of those who witnessed them.

SOURCES

7 Edvard Radzinsky, *Stalin* (New York: Anchor, 1997), 17.
8 Ibid., 24.
8 Simon Sebag Montefiore, *Stalin: The Court of the Red Tsar* (New York: Alfred A. Knopf, 2004), 26.
8 Radzinsky, *Stalin*, 25.
13 Ibid., 28.
13 Robert Conquest, *Stalin: Breaker of Nations* (New York: Penguin, 1991), 13.
13 Radzinsky, *Stalin*, 32.
13 Ibid., 33.
13 Ibid.
13 Ibid., 36.
15 Ibid.
15–16 Harold Shukman, *Stalin* (Phoenix Mill, UK: Sutton, 1999), 7.
16 Radzinsky, *Stalin*, 35.
16 Ibid., 64.
16 Shukman, *Stalin*, 14.
20 Orlando Figes, *A People's Tragedy: A History of the Russian Revolution* (New York: Viking, 1996), 307.
21 Radzinsky, *Stalin*, 88.
21 Figes, *A People's Tragedy*, 315.
25 Radzinsky, *Stalin*, 97.
25 Ibid., 99.
28 Ibid., 121.
28 Ibid., 128.
30 Ibid., 153.
31 Ibid., 152.
32 Ibid. 153.
33 Martin Amis, *Koba the Dread: Laughter and the Twenty Million* (New York: Vintage International, 2002), 30.
36 Radzinsky, *Stalin*. 35.
40 Conquest, *Stalin: Breaker of Nations*, 100.
40 Shukman, *Stalin*, 57.
40 Conquest, *Stalin: Breaker of Nations*, 101.
42 Radzinsky, *Stalin*, 200–201.

43 Conquest, *Stalin: Breaker of Nations*, 103.
47 Radzinsky, *Stalin*, 202.
47 Conquest, *Stalin: Breaker of Nations*, 104.
47 Ibid., 135.
48 Sebag Montefiore. *Stalin: The Court of the Red Tsar*, 8.
48 Ibid., 8.
48 Conquest, *Stalin: Breaker of Nations*, 128.
54 Ibid., 153.
55 Ibid.
55 Ibid., 154.
55 Ibid., 152.
55 Ibid., 154.
57 Richard Overy, *Russia's War: A History of the Soviet War Effort, 1941–1945* (New York: Penguin, 1998), 1.
57 Robert Conquest, *The Harvest of Sorrow: Soviet Collectivization and the Terror-Famine* (New York: Oxford University Press, 1986), 89.
58 Conquest, *Stalin: Breaker of Nations*, 158.
58 Conquest, *Harvest of Sorrow*, 223.
58 Sebag Montefiore, *Stalin: The Court of the Red Tsar*, 7.
59 Ibid., 17.
62 Ibid., 21.
63 Ibid., 22.
64 Conquest, *Stalin: Breaker of Nations*, 169.
65 Conquest, *Harvest of Sorrow*, 261.
65 Radzinsky, *Stalin*, 305.
66 Shukman, *Stalin*, 79.
66 Ibid.
66 Radzinsky. *Stalin*, 321.
67 Conquest, *Harvest of Sorrow*, 248.
67 Ibid., 258.
67 Ibid., 230.
68 Radzinsky. *Stalin*, 326.
68 Robert Conquest. *The Great Terror: A Reassessment* (New York: Oxford University Press, 1990), 48.
68 *Russia's War: Blood upon the Snow. Episode 1: The Darkness Descends*. Directed by Viktor Lisakovitch. PBS Home Video, 1997.

71   Conquest, *Stalin: Breaker of Nations*, 220.
74   Ibid., 221.
75   Ibid., 235.
76   Sebag Montefiore, *Stalin: The Court of the Red Tsar*, 374.
79   Ibid.
81   Ibid.
83   Ibid.
85   Ibid., 378.
85   Conquest, *Stalin: Breaker of Nations*, 251.
86   Amis, *Koba the Dread*, 173.
86   Conquest, *Stalin: Breaker of Nations*, 310.
86   Ibid., 278.
86   Radzinsky, *Stalin*, 556.
89   Conquest, *Stalin: Breaker of Nations*, 314.
95   Amis, *Koba the Dread*, 49.
95   Conquest, *Stalin: Breaker of Nations*, 310.
97   Ibid., 278.
98   Radzinsky, *Stalin*, 556.
101   Conquest, *Stalin: Breaker of Nations*, 314.
102   Amis, *Koba the Dread*, 49.

Selected Bibliography

Amis, Martin. *Koba the Dread: Laughter and the Twenty Million.* New York: Vintage International, 2002.

Conquest, Robert. *The Great Terror: A Reassessment.* New York: Oxford University Press, 1990.

———. *The Harvest of Sorrow: Soviet Collectivization and the Terror-Famine.* New York: Oxford University Press, 1986.

———. *Stalin: Breaker of Nations.* New York: Penguin, 1991.

Figes, Orlando. *A People's Tragedy: A History of the Russian Revolution.* New York: Viking, 1996.

Freeze, Gregory. *Russia: A History.* New York: Oxford University Press, 1997.

Hochschild, Adam. *The Unquiet Ghost: Russians Remember Stalin.* Boston: Mariner, 2003.

Medvedev, Roy. *Let History Judge: The Origins and Consequences of Stalinism.* Rev. ed. New York: Columbia University Press, 1989.

Overy, Richard. *Russia's War: A History of the Soviet War Effort, 1941–1945.* New York: Penguin, 1998.

Radzinsky, Edvard. *Stalin.* New York: Anchor, 1997.

Read, Christopher, ed. *The Stalin Years: A Reader.* New York: Palgrave Macmillan, 2003.

Sebag Montefiore, Simon. *Stalin: The Court of the Red Tsar.* New York: Alfred A. Knopf, 2004.

Shukman, Harold. *Stalin.* Phoenix Mill, UK: Sutton, 1999.

Westwood, J. N. *Endurance and Endeavor: Russian History, 1812–1992.* 4th ed. New York: Oxford University Press, 1993.

FURTHER READING AND WEBSITES

BOOKS

Feldman, Ruth Tenzer. *World War I*. Minneapolis: Lerner Publications Company, 2005.

Goldstein, Margaret J. *World War II—Europe*. Minneapolis: Lerner Publications Company, 2004.

Gottfried, Ted. *The Road to Communism*. Minneapolis: Twenty-First Century Books, 2002.

———. *The Stalinist Empire*. Minneapolis: Twenty-First Century Books, 2002.

Heyes, Eileen. *Adolf Hitler*. Brookfield, CT: Millbrook Press, 1994.

Koestler, Arthur. *Darkness at Noon*, New York: Bantam Books, 1984.

Kort, Michael G. *The Handbook of the Former Soviet Union*. Minneapolis: Millbrook Press, 1997.

———. *Marxism in Power*. Brookfield, CT: Millbrook Press, 1993.

Lazo, Caroline Evensen. *Harry S. Truman*. Minneapolis: Lerner Publications Company, 2003.

Márquez, Herón. *Russia in Pictures*. Minneapolis: Lerner Publications Company, 2004.

Orwell, George. *Animal Farm*. New York: Signet, 2004.

———. *1984*. New York: Signet, 1990.

Plotkin, Gregory, and Rita Plotkin. *Cooking the Russian Way*. Minneapolis: Lerner Publications Company, 2003.

Rius. *Marx for Beginners*. New York: Pantheon, 2003.

Roberts, Jeremy. *Franklin D. Roosevelt*. Minneapolis: Lerner Publications Company, 2003.

Sherman, Josepha. *The Cold War*. Minneapolis: Lerner Publications Company, 2004.

Streissguth, Tom. *Life in Communist Russia*. San Diego: Lucent, 2001.

Toht, Patricia. *Daily Life in Ancient and Modern Moscow*. Minneapolis: Lerner Publications Company, 2001.

The American Relief Administration in Soviet Russia
   http://www-hoover.stanford.edu/hila/ara.htm. Part of a Hoover
   Tower Rotunda Exhibit from the Hoover Institution Library
   and Archives website, this page contains information on the
   American Relief Administration in Russia, as well as primary
   source documents and photographs.

Hitler and Stalin
   http://library.thinkquest.org/19092. This website provides
   information on both Adolf Hitler and Joseph Stalin. Pages
   are dedicated to different periods in their lifetimes and
   provide a variety of biography information, including photos.
   Headings include "The Early Years," "Struggle for Power,"
   "End of Regime," and more.

Stalin Biographical Chronicle
   http://www.stel.ru/stalin. This website organizes Joseph
   Stalin's life into a series of timelines. Clear and concise
   information contains links to related material.

INDEX

OTHER TITLES FROM LERNER AND A&E®:

Arnold Schwarzenegger
Ariel Sharon
Arthur Ashe
The Beatles
Benito Mussolini
Benjamin Franklin
Bill Gates
Bruce Lee
Carl Sagan
Chief Crazy Horse
Christopher Reeve
Colin Powell
Daring Pirate Women
Edgar Allan Poe
Eleanor Roosevelt
Fidel Castro
Frank Gehry
George Lucas
George W. Bush
Gloria Estefan
Hillary Rodham Clinton
Jack London
Jacques Cousteau
Jane Austen
Jesse Owens
Jesse Ventura
Jimi Hendrix
J. K. Rowling
John Glenn
Latin Sensations
Legends of Dracula

Legends of Santa Claus
Louisa May Alcott
Madeleine Albright
Malcolm X
Mao Zedung
Mark Twain
Maya Angelou
Mohandas Gandhi
Mother Teresa
Napoleon Bonaparte
Nelson Mandela
Oprah Winfrey
Osama bin Laden
Pope John Paul II
Princess Diana
Queen Cleopatra
Queen Elizabeth I
Queen Latifah
Rosie O'Donnell
Saddam Hussein
Saint Joan of Arc
Thurgood Marshall
Tiger Woods
Tony Blair
Vladimir Putin
William Shakespeare
Wilma Rudolph
Winston Churchill
Women in Space
Women of the Wild West
Yasser Arafat

ABOUT THE AUTHOR

Jeffrey Zuehlke is a writer and editor. He has written more than a dozen books for young readers, including *Poland in Pictures, Ukraine in Pictures, Germany in Pictures,* and *Jordan in Pictures.* He lives in Minneapolis.

PHOTO ACKNOWLEDGMENTS

The images in this book are used with the permission of: © Brown Brothers, pp. 2, 9, 17, 18, 22, 26, 50, 60, 100; © Bettmann/CORBIS, pp. 6, 41, 64, 72, 75; © CORBIS, pp. 10, 69; © Getty Images, pp. 12, 14, 33, 53, 77, 83, 84, 94; The Illustrated London News, p. 29; © SuperStock, Inc./SuperStock, p. 34; Library of Congress, pp. 42 (LC-USZ62-95141), 62 (LC-USF345-091138-A), 88 (LC-USZ62-073335); © KPA/ZUMA Press, p. 44; © United States Holocaust Memorial Museum, p. 70; © Yevgeny Khaldei/CORBIS, p. 91; © Independent Picture Service, p. 92.

Front cover: © Bettmann/Corbis. Back cover: Library of Congress (LC-USW33-019081).

WEBSITES

Website addresses in this book were valid at the time of printing. However, because of the nature of the Internet, some addresses may have changed or sites may have closed since publication. While the author and Publisher regret any inconvenience this may cause readers, no responsibility for any such changes can be accepted by the author or Publisher.